COURTING HISTORY

Freedom of the Press

Crown v. John Peter Zenger

JEANNE MARIE FORD

Cavendish Square

New York

Published in 2019 by Cavendish Square Publishing, LLC
243 5th Avenue, Suite 136, New York, NY 10016

Library of Congress Cataloging-in-Publication Data

Names: Ford, Jeanne Marie, 1971- author.
Title: Freedom of the press : Crown v. John Peter Zenger / Jeanne Marie Ford.
Description: New York : Cavendish Square, 2018. |
Series: Courting history | Includes bibliographical references and index.
Identifiers: LCCN 2017061441 (print) | LCCN 2018000744 (ebook) |
ISBN 9781502635846 (eBook) | ISBN 9781502635839 (library bound) |
ISBN 9781502635853 (pbk.)
Subjects: LCSH: Zenger, John Peter, 1697-1746--Trials, litigation, etc.--Juvenile literature. |
Freedom of the press--New York (State)--Juvenile literature. |
Freedom of the press--United States--History--Juvenile literature. |
Trials (Seditious libel)--New York (State)--New York--Juvenile literature.
Classification: LCC KF223.Z4 (ebook) | LCC KF223.Z4 F67 2018 (print) |
DDC 342.74708/53--dc23
LC record available at https://lccn.loc.gov/2017061441

Editorial Director: David McNamara
Editor: Chet'la Sebree
Copy Editor: Nathan Heidelberger
Associate Art Director: Amy Greenan
Designer: Joseph Parenteau
Production Coordinator: Karol Szymczuk
Photo Research: J8 Media

Printed in the United States of America

Contents

ONE
Newspapers and Colonial New York

In June 1710, almost thirteen-year-old John Peter Zenger disembarked from a ship in New York Harbor and stepped onto the first land he'd seen in months. Nearly five hundred of his fellow German immigrants had died on the risky voyage to America. Zenger's father was among them. After his father's death, his family faced a new life in a strange land with no money and no means of support.

John Peter Zenger traveled from Germany to New York in 1710. This illustration, from 1798, captures a likeness of his first view of the city.

Colonial New York

The Dutch were the first settlers in New York, which they named New Amsterdam. The British changed the city's name to New York when they seized it in 1664. Once the British had taken over the city, they implemented their own governmental system.

The colony was ruled by the colonial governor, who was selected by the British monarch, or the country's king or queen. The colonial governor had much more power than state governors do today. The governor appointed members of the Provincial Council and most government officials, including judges, sheriffs, and tax collectors. He served as military commander, or leader, and also chose the mayors of the colony's two largest settlements, New York City and Albany.

The legislative, or lawmaking, branch of the colony, called the General Assembly, was elected by New York's citizens. However, the assembly members could meet only with the governor's permission. The governor could also veto, or reject, any bill they passed. Additionally, the governor served as the chief judge of the New York Court of Chancery, or the court of equity. The court of equity was the court that dealt with lawsuits and petitions. In this way, the governor had a great deal of control over the colony—for better or for worse.

Freedom of the Press:
Crown v. John Peter Zenger

The British took control of the Dutch city of New Amsterdam in 1664 and renamed it New York.

As Zenger's family sailed westward, the new colonial governor of New York, Robert Hunter, was making the same trip on a more luxurious ship. Fortunately for Zenger and his family, Hunter was an honest and honorable man. He had promised England's Queen Anne that he would help the new settlers find housing and jobs. He kept his word.

By October 1710, Zenger had secured an eight-year position as an apprentice, or a person who is learning a skilled job from a master of a certain trade, for William Bradford. Bradford was the official and only royal printer in the colony of New York. In exchange for room and board, Zenger would serve as Bradford's assistant and learn his trade.

Printing and Libel Laws

The printing press was invented in 1439. It was a machine that transferred ink, which made creating multiple copies of printed material easier. With the invention of the printing press, the ruling class quickly realized the power of the written word to spread new ideas.

Even with the printing press, running a print shop was not an easy way to make a living in colonial America. After

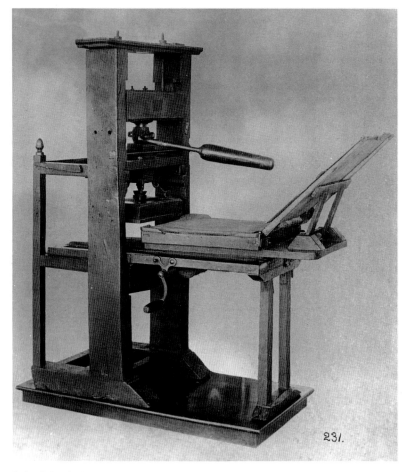

Colonial printing presses were operated by hand.

one hundred years of settlement in the colonies, only fifteen print shops had been opened. There were a number of difficulties involved with opening a print shop. The tools of the trade were expensive and difficult to obtain. Additionally, ingredients to make ink had to be imported from Europe, and American-made paper was generally of poor quality.

All of these difficulties aside, the biggest obstacle to running a successful print shop was the British government. The British Parliament, or the lawmaking branch of the British government, controlled everything from what types of fonts could be used to what content could be printed. In 1529, King Henry VIII began to exercise strict control over the press. He issued a list of banned books. He forbade anyone except for the licensed royal printer to operate presses. Printers who published unapproved works could be taken to trial.

In 1487, Britain's Court of Star Chamber was established. It was a legal body that operated outside of the regular court system. The court also took a stance on what could be said about the government. It defined libel as written criticism of the government. Seditious libel, or written criticism of the government meant to encourage rebellion, was the most serious type of offense involving the written word. The government believed that criticism threatened its authority as well as peace and order. Under older laws, a spoken or written claim had to be false in order for it to be considered slander or libel. The Star Chamber changed this definition. The court did not consider truth to be a legal defense against slander or libel. In fact, a true claim was thought to be a more serious offense because a truthful critique of the government was more likely to encourage rebellion.

Although the Star Chamber was abolished in 1641, people were still prosecuted using its definition of libel. In

these cases, the court system's judges were responsible for deciding whether or not published works were libelous. In other words, they were responsible for deciding whether or not the works criticized the government. The only job of the jurors was to determine whether or not the accused had printed the materials in question. In 1695, printer licensing laws, which required each printer to get permission before printing any material, ended in England. Although those laws were no longer active, censorship, or the prohibition of certain material, remained common. Only members of Parliament could say whatever they wished without fear of prosecution.

William Bradford, Royal Printer

A British immigrant, William Bradford had begun his printing career in the colony of Pennsylvania. He quickly managed to anger members of the Provincial Council, who served at the governor's pleasure. He angered them by printing the colony's original charter, a document that defined the rights of the colony's citizens. The governor told Bradford that, in the future, he should not print anything without his permission. Bradford responded that "printing is a manufacture of the nation, and therefore ought rather to be encouraged than suppressed." In other words, Bradford believed that documents like Pennsylvania's charter were important to the colonists. Since they were important, he thought the distribution of such information through printing should be encouraged.

After he printed pamphlets expressing views that mildly opposed the government, Bradford was held in jail for four months before he was granted a jury trial. In court, he tried to argue that the jury should be able to decide whether or

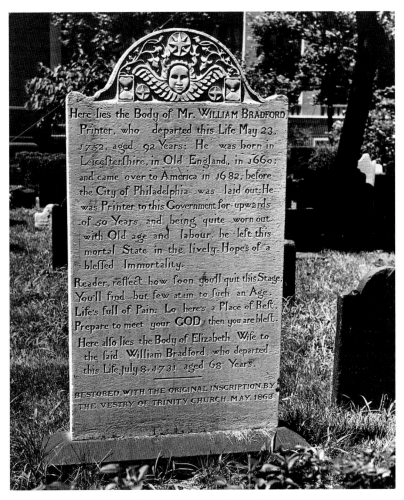

Printer William Bradford is buried at the Trinity Church graveyard, on New York City's Wall Street.

not what he printed was true. The judge did not allow this. Ultimately, the only defense Bradford could offer was that there was no proof that he had published the materials in question. In court, the jurors passed the printing press's letters, which were evidence, around the room. The letters were accidentally destroyed in this process. As a result, the

jury could not come to a decision, and the case was dismissed. When Bradford was released from prison, he decided to move to New York at the invitation of its governor. By the time he took on Zenger as his apprentice, his business was doing well.

Zenger Comes of Age

After his apprenticeship with Bradford was complete, twenty-one-year-old John Peter Zenger moved to Philadelphia. While there, he briefly worked with Bradford's son, Andrew. Zenger then married and relocated to Maryland with hopes of becoming that colony's official printer. Unfortunately, he was never hired as the official printer, and his wife died in childbirth. In search of a fresh start, Zenger returned to New York. He remarried and started working for Bradford again.

In 1725, Bradford began New York's first newspaper, the *New-York Gazette*. It was one of the only newspapers printed in the colonies at the time. One of the first had been published by Bradford's son in Philadelphia. Another, Boston's *New-England Courant*, was founded by Benjamin Franklin's older brother, James. As a teenager, Benjamin Franklin published his own column in the *Courant* under a pseudonym, or fake name. Both Andrew Bradford and James Franklin ultimately faced criminal charges over controversial material they published. William Bradford was clearly aware that he must be careful not to offend the government. His articles avoided any topics to which the governor might object. As a result, the newspaper had few subscribers.

In 1726, Zenger decided to try starting his own business again. He opened a shop across the street from the popular Black Horse Tavern. His print shop would be a direct competitor of Bradford's. While he was more successful than

he'd been in Maryland, he still struggled to get enough work to make ends meet. Ultimately, his concerns about money may have influenced his decision to take on the controversial printing jobs Bradford did not want.

Governor William Cosby

In 1732, a new royal governor, William Cosby, was appointed by King George II. Upon arriving in New York, Cosby quickly made enemies among the colony's most powerful residents. Respected Provincial Council member Rip Van Dam had served as acting governor while the colonists waited for Cosby to arrive from England. Cosby insisted that Van Dam should pay him half the salary he had earned during this period. When Van Dam refused to agree to this demand, Cosby sued him.

Since Van Dam was popular among the colonists, Cosby knew he was unlikely to win a jury trial. He wanted the Supreme Court of Judicature of the Province of New York to hear the case. This was unusual because the Supreme Court usually handled cases dealing with the law as opposed to lawsuits or disputes. The case would typically have been heard by the New York Court of Chancery. It could not be heard by that court, however, because Cosby served as its head judge. Legally, he could not make a ruling on his own lawsuit. The crafty Cosby decided to use his power to renew an expired law that allowed a Supreme Court hearing without a jury. The Supreme Court's chief justice, or head judge, Lewis Morris, was a good friend of Van Dam's. However, the other two judges, James DeLancey and Frederick Philipse II, were Morris's enemies. Cosby was almost certain they would side with him.

TWO

Crown v. John Peter Zenger

Justice Morris was furious that Governor Cosby would use his power to bypass the established legal system in the 1733 *Cosby v. Van Dam* case. In his frustration, Morris went behind Justices DeLancey and Philipse's backs to work with Van Dam's attorney, James Alexander. Morris and Alexander made a plan to sabotage Cosby's lawsuit. Their plan was both unethical and illegal. Fortunately for them, the two men were not caught.

Morris wrote a legal opinion, or written legal explanation, about Cosby's plan to have his case tried without a jury. Morris had his opinion printed by John Peter Zenger's shop and distributed to the colony's residents as a pamphlet. As a result, public opinion began to grow against Cosby. DeLancey and Philipse felt the political pressure from the people. The inexperienced Philipse, who had been made a judge as a favor to his wealthy family, asked for more time to consider the matter. Despite his loyalty to Cosby, DeLancey felt he had no choice but to recuse, or excuse, himself from the case.

Cosby's lawsuit was officially in limbo, or in an unresolved state. As an act of revenge, he removed Morris from the position of chief justice and promoted DeLancey. Morris and Alexander saw this action as yet another bold abuse of the governor's power. They were determined to make sure this abuse of power did not go unchallenged. They approached Zenger again. This time they asked Zenger about printing a

Numb. L.

THE

New - York Weekly JOURNAL.

Containing the freſheſt Advices, Foreign, and Domeſtick.

MUNDAY October 14th, 1734.

Mr. *Zenger*;

I Have been Reading, the arguments of Mr. *Smith*, and *Murray*, with Regard to the Courts, and there is one Thing, I can't comprehend, *viz*. If it is the ſame Court, I take it, that all the Writs ought to be taken out in *England*, and teſted by the Judges there; if they are taken out here, the ſame Judges ought to teſt them here. If it is a like Court, it is not the ſame; and if not the ſame, it is not that fundamental Court which is eſtabliſhed by immemorial Cuſtom. I would be glad ſome of your Correſpondents would clear up this Point; becauſe in my poor Oppinion, if the Exchequer Court here is not the ſame identical Court as the Exchequer Court in *England*, it is without Lawful Authority.

⬛⬛⬛⬛ ⬛⬛ ⬛⬛⬛⬛⬛

FOREIGN AFFAIRS.

Dantzick, Auguſt 4.

Yeſterday the Biſhop of Cracow, in the King's Name, received Homage of this City, and the Ceremony was very magnificent. His Majeſty, before his Departure, iſſued the Univerſalia for holding of the Petty-Dyets in the Provinces. Thoſe in Poliſh Pruſſia, will be held in 15 Days. The Ruſſian and Saxon Troops will march ſuddenly to the Places where the Provincial Aſſemblies are to be opened; and the reſt are to go and poſt them-

ſelves in Great Poland. M. Rewuſki, the Crown Carver, is declared Regimentary, and is to command a Body of Troops, conſiſting of 2000 Ruſſian Dragoons, 11000 Coſſacks, and the Regiment Guards formerly in the Service of King Staniſlaus.

Bruſſels, Auguſt 6.

Letters from Rome of the 17th paſt advile. That they had Advice there that the Siege of Gaeta was not yet formed, altho' the Spaniards had there 70 Cannon, and Mortars, and were working on Batteries, but that all they raiſed in the Night was beat down next Morning by the Cannon of the Palace; and that the Heats being already Exceſſive, the Spaniards were in Fear of looſing a vaſt Number of Men in the Reduction of that Fortreſs.

Hamburg, Auguſt 10.

According to Letters from the Camp before Dantzick, the Veſſels there were taken up by Order of the Generals in Chief, to ſerve for carrying the heavy Artillery and Baggage by Water to Thorn and Warſaw.

We have certain Advice, that King, Staniſlaus was departed from Brandenburg Pruſſia, and arrived ſafe in the Crown Army, under the Command of M. Kiowſki, near Peterkow the 24th paſt, and immediately afterwards held a Council of War, wherein it was reſolved to draw all the diſperſed Troops into a Body, and march directly to Volhinia in Podolia.

Amſt.

Zenger began publishing the *New-York Weekly Journal* in 1733.

newspaper that would expose the governor's corruption. They believed that the press was the most efficient way to destroy Cosby's career and force the appointment of a new royal governor.

The *New-York Weekly Journal*

In 1733, Zenger published the first edition of the *New-York Weekly Journal*. Cosby knew that Morris and Alexander were the anonymous, or nameless, authors of its content. However, he had no way of proving their involvement, so it would be almost impossible to bring charges against them. Zenger, on the other hand, was the printer of record. His name appeared on the newspaper's masthead. On January 15, 1734, Cosby had Chief Justice DeLancey assemble a grand jury to charge Zenger with seditious libel. The grand jury would decide whether or not the case went to trial.

There was no question that the articles Zenger printed met the legal definition of seditious libel: "the intentional publication, without lawful excuse or justification, of written blame of any public man or of the law, or any institution established by the law." In other words, any public criticism of the law or a public figure, like the governor, was against the law, even if it was true. Cosby thought the royal government (also known as the Crown) would have an open and shut case against Zenger.

The Case Against William Cosby

Zenger's paper had quickly gained popularity among the residents of New York City. Meanwhile, the governor grew increasingly unpopular as claims of his bad behavior were revealed in the *New-York Weekly Journal*. The newspaper's first

edition had announced the victory of Lewis Morris for a seat in the General Assembly. The article claimed that Governor Cosby had tried to take Morris out of the running. Cosby questioned whether or not thirty-eight of Morris's Quaker supporters had the right to vote. The sheriff required them to swear on the Bible that they were legally eligible to vote. The sheriff knew that their religion prohibited them from swearing oaths. Since Morris's Quaker supporters could not swear an oath, they were not allowed to vote. Although they were unfairly disqualified from voting, Morris still won with 231 votes to his challenger's 151.

Other issues of the newspaper accused Cosby of taking land for his own benefit and befriending the French, who were bitter enemies of the British. Due to their personal grudge against Cosby, Morris and Alexander likely painted him in the worst possible light. Even so, their reporting was based in fact. The pieces they published in the *Journal* also frequently defended the freedom of speech and a free press.

This mid-eighteenth-century image demonstrates how colonial trials were full of British pomp. Lawyers and judges wore powdered wigs.

Zenger Goes Before the Grand Jury

Many of the grand jury members seated in Zenger's trial had been reading these articles for weeks. Likely swayed by their content, they declined to indict, or formally charge, Zenger. The *Journal*'s January 28, 1734, issue listed all nineteen of the jurors' names and thanked them for their "tender concerns for the liberties of their fellow citizens." Essentially, the newspaper thanked them for protecting Zenger's ability to publish the truth.

Inspired by their victory, Alexander and Morris used the next issue of the *Journal* to attack corrupt governors. While they never mentioned Cosby by name, their meaning was clear. Meanwhile, the *Gazette*, Bradford's paper, began publishing articles defending Cosby and attacking Zenger. The *Gazette* writers argued against the idea that the press was a necessary way of preserving the people's freedom.

Zenger's Second Hearing

To celebrate the victory of several Cosby opponents in the September 1734 New York City Common Council elections, Zenger published pamphlets filled with celebratory songs that poked fun at the governor. Cosby's anger grew as New Yorkers walked the streets singing insults about him. He again pressed for libel charges to be filed against Zenger. Chief Justice DeLancey asked a new grand jury to indict Zenger. He told them it was their duty to identify whoever wrote the songs and prosecute him to the fullest extent of the law.

Five of the nineteen jurors selected had served on the previous grand jury that declined to indict Zenger. They were no more motivated to find Zenger guilty now. They claimed

Cosby's Government

Only white male landowners were eligible to vote in colonial elections. They were a small portion of the population. Many rich New York landowners were friends and loyal to Governor Cosby and the Crown. The rising middle class, however, tended to support Morris.

With Morris's 1733 General Assembly victory, his pro-colonist group was close to gaining the majority of the assembly's seats. When the legislative body was in session, Morris offered a number of bills designed to reduce Cosby's authority. While these bills had no chance of passing, Morris employed every method he knew to upset the governor. For example, he wrote an essay published anonymously in the *Journal* titled "Observations on James DeLancey's Charge." In it, he criticized the chief justice, whom Cosby had appointed in his place, as unqualified. He claimed that DeLancey was merely the governor's puppet.

Since Cosby's supporters just barely made up the majority of the colony's General Assembly, Cosby did not allow new assembly elections. He was afraid new elections might result in his allies losing seats. He could not, however, stop the New York City Common Council from holding elections that September. Morris's supporters won six of the seven council seats.

it was impossible to determine who had authored or printed the pamphlet. They were clearly looking for an excuse not to charge Zenger since he was the only printer in the colony who wasn't working for the governor. There was no real question in anyone's mind that he had printed the pamphlet.

Cosby knew that his support from the public would only continue to diminish if Zenger continued publishing the *Journal*. Rather than dropping the case after two grand juries had refused to indict Zenger, Cosby offered a reward of fifty pounds for proof against the pamphlet's publishers. He then pushed his Provincial Council to declare that Zenger's newspapers should be publicly burned. The city's newly elected officials were ordered to attend the event. They refused. They also would not allow the city's hangman to carry out the governor's request. The sheriff's servant ultimately had to burn the papers himself.

Zenger's Arrest

At this point, Cosby decided that the only way to prevent further damage to his reputation was to stop the presses altogether. He used his power to go around the grand jury's verdict. He had an arrest warrant issued for Zenger on charges of seditious libel. On November 17, 1734, the sheriff locked Zenger in a jail cell at City Hall to await trial.

Alexander, one of the best lawyers in the colony, immediately filed a writ of habeas corpus, or a document requesting an explanation for someone's imprisonment. He also challenged the legality of the arrest. He argued that Zenger's offense, if any, was a misdemeanor, or a minor crime. For that reason, Alexander believed that Zenger's bail should be set at an amount he could afford to pay.

Zenger's newspapers were publicly burned on Wall Street in November 1734.

Chief Justice DeLancey, who presided over the bail hearing, had been desperate to get Zenger behind bars for months. Unsurprisingly, he had no mercy for the printer. In fact, he declared in open court that a jury would be forced to find Zenger guilty. He set bail at eight hundred pounds,

an amount far too high for Zenger to pay. Alexander was wealthy enough that he likely could have put up money for Zenger's bail. However, he knew Zenger would get sympathy from the public if he remained in prison. Meanwhile, Zenger refused to name Alexander and Morris as the anonymous authors of the articles.

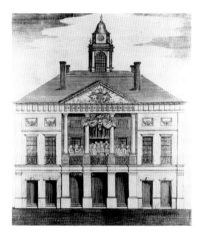

Zenger was held in a jail cell in New York's Old City Hall.

Zenger's imprisonment only kept the *Journal* out of print for one week. On November 25, it resumed publication. Zenger's wife, Anna, and two of their teenaged sons ran the presses while Morris and Alexander continued writing their criticism of Governor Cosby. Zenger was able to communicate with Anna through a hole in the door of his cell as he awaited trial.

When the Supreme Court's term expired in January, yet another grand jury was assembled to hear Zenger's case. While no records of the proceeding itself survive, the verdict was the same as the previous two. After Zenger was cleared for a third time, he expected that he would finally be released. Cosby had other plans. He took advantage of a rare procedure called an "information." This procedure allowed the government to order a case to proceed to trial without an indictment, or charge. While many New Yorkers viewed such a move as an abuse of power, Cosby saw it as the only option for him to keep his power.

THREE

Truth as a Defense Against Libel

Zenger's hearing could not begin until the Supreme Court's spring term opened in April 1735. His lawyer, James Alexander, took advantage of the court's break to plan a defense. He knew it would be nearly impossible to convincingly claim that Zenger had not printed the materials that had been entered into evidence. Instead, he planned to argue that publishing antigovernment articles should not be illegal in the first place.

The Legal Definition of Libel

Alexander believed that British law remained unsettled regarding the legal definition of libel. British officials generally made few arrests on charges of seditious libel. Typically, the threat of being arrested was enough to keep publishers from printing anything the government might find objectionable.

The "Cato" Essays

Beginning in 1720, British journalists John Trenchard and Thomas Gordon tested the limits of press freedom. They wrote a series of 144 published essays under the pen name

This undated engraving illustrates the courtroom during one of John Peter Zenger's trials.

"Cato." These essays were read widely in both England and America. They argued that freedom of speech was a fundamental freedom, as long as it did not violate others' rights. "Cato" wrote, "In those wretched countries where a man cannot call his tongue his own, he can scarcely call anything else his own." In other words, what can a man own if not his own words?

Alexander admired Trenchard and Gordon's ideas and published several of the "Cato" essays in the *Journal*. The "Cato" essays argued that the people, not the government, should decide whether published material portrayed its subjects in a fair light. Trenchard and Gordon agreed that it was defamation to damage someone's reputation by making untrue accusations. They agreed that this should indeed be illegal. On the other hand, they believed that printing the truth, even if it portrayed someone negatively, should be legal because it served an important function in society.

For months, Alexander used the articles in the *Journal* to persuade New Yorkers—including potential jury members—that Zenger's actions should not be against the law.

Richard Francklin and the *Craftsman*

Alexander knew that recent cases posed real legal danger to Zenger. Inspired by the "Cato" essays, British journalists had become more daring in publishing antigovernment writing. For example, Richard Francklin began publishing a journal called the *Craftsman* in London in 1726. He was indicted five years later for seeking to "vilify the administration of his current majesty's government."

Francklin's defense attorney asked jurors to consider whether the government officials "deserved to have such things said of them." The judge, unmoved by this defense, ordered the jury to return a "special verdict." This instruction meant that jurors could consider only certain facts of the case. The judge had already determined that Francklin's writing was libelous. He told the jurors it was not up to them to consider whether or not the newspaper was fair or truthful. If Francklin had published the issue in question, then they must find him guilty. The jury did as the judge ordered. Francklin was sentenced to a year in prison and was required to pay a fine to ensure that he would not print any more objectionable material.

Alexander Plans Zenger's Defense

Francklin's case was at the forefront of Alexander's mind as he prepared Zenger's defense. His notes from early 1735 show that he was ready to challenge any order from the judge to return a special verdict. Alexander was prepared to argue

England's Court of Star Chamber took its name from the stars that decorated the room's ceiling.

that the judge could not limit which facts the jury could consider. He believed that the jurors, not the judge, should be the ones to decide whether or not Zenger was guilty.

Alexander's main strategy was to question the common law definition of criminal libel. The original British laws

against slander, dating back to 1275, had placed limits only on speech that was false. While the Star Chamber did not allow truth to serve as a defense against libel, that court had been abolished nearly a century before. Although its libel laws were still in effect, Alexander believed that the laws should be revisited. As he had written in the *Journal*, he believed that the law should not be used to protect a corrupt government. He planned to argue that government officials should be the ones prosecuted if they broke the law, not the journalists who exposed the truth.

While Alexander felt that he had a strong argument, he also knew he had a difficult obstacle to overcome in the courtroom. Chief Justice DeLancey would be one of two judges hearing the case. The third seat remained empty since Morris was dismissed in 1733. DeLancey was one of Cosby's most loyal allies. He had already urged three grand juries to indict Zenger. For these reasons, Alexander did not believe DeLancey could oversee a fair trial. He considered asking the chief justice to recuse himself from the case due to his obvious bias. However, he was afraid this strategy might backfire. If this strategy did not work, Alexander would embarrass DeLancey. An embarrassed DeLancey might be even more prejudiced, or biased, against Zenger. Ultimately, Alexander decided to take a slightly different approach.

Disbarred

Alexander filed a motion to challenge whether DeLancey and Philipse were allowed to sit on the court following Morris's dismissal. Alexander and his co-counsel, or supporting lawyer, William Smith, argued that Cosby had violated the law by failing to put the justices' appointments through the appropriate approval process.

DeLancey believed this motion challenged both the validity, or legality, of the justices' appointments and the court itself. He asked Zenger's attorneys whether they were certain they wanted to proceed with their objection. Alexander and Smith said yes. DeLancey said he would consider the matter overnight.

The next day, DeLancey told the attorneys that they had brought the case "to the point that either we [DeLancey and Philipse] must go from the bench, or you from the bar." With this statement, DeLancey meant that either the justices could no longer serve as justices or the attorneys could no longer serve as attorneys. He followed through with his statement by disbarring Alexander and Smith. This meant that DeLancey was taking away both lawyers' rights to practice law.

DeLancey disbarring Alexander and Smith meant that Zenger had lost his attorneys and his most devoted defenders.

Lewis Morris was in London during Zenger's trial. An eighteenth-century rendering of the city is featured here.

Without a good legal defense in court, Zenger would likely lose his trial. Lewis Morris was the most logical person to step in as his attorney. He was both qualified and motivated. Unfortunately, Morris was in London pursuing his plan to have Cosby removed from his position as royal governor.

Zenger was forced to ask DeLancey to name a court-appointed attorney to represent him. The chief justice chose John Chambers, a young lawyer who had been known to support Cosby in the past. Chambers entered a not-guilty plea, or a formal statement of innocence, for Zenger. He then requested more time to prepare Zenger's defense. The trial was rescheduled for early August. Zenger continued to wait in jail for his trial.

Alexander and Smith tried to coach Chambers on how to prepare the best defense for Zenger. Chambers ignored their advice. Alexander worried about Chambers's inexperience and possible lack of concern for the case. He began to look for a more capable attorney for Zenger.

Alexander soon found that New York's best lawyers were unwilling to take on Zenger's case. They were afraid of angering Governor Cosby. After Alexander had difficulty finding a replacement lawyer, he started writing statements for Zenger to memorize and recite himself when his hearing started.

Jury Selection

Chambers, meanwhile, made a move in Zenger's interest. He requested a "struck jury," a jury selected from a random group of New Yorkers rather than chosen by Cosby's sheriff.

Cosby had other ideas. As jury selection began in August, his sheriff created a list of forty-eight possible jurors. Their

names had supposedly been taken from a pool of thousands of landowners. Chambers quickly realized that these jurors had not been selected at random. On the list of jurors were Cosby's baker, his candlemaker, and his tailor, among many of his friends and associates. Chambers objected to the attempt to fill the jury with Cosby supporters. DeLancey ruled in his favor. He ordered that the sheriff's list be discarded and demanded a truly fair jury selection process. DeLancey did not want to run the risk of anyone questioning the legality of the trial.

The prosecuting attorney was Attorney General Richard Bradley. An attorney general is the head lawyer for a government. Bradley and Chambers each had the opportunity to object to twelve names on the new list that the court created. Finally, they chose their twelve jurors. The foreman, or head juror, was Thomas Hunt, a mariner. He and at least five other jurors were believed to be Morris supporters. Zenger's prospects seemed to be improving. However, he still lacked an experienced lawyer, and the law was not on his side.

The Trial Begins

The trial began on a Monday, which was the day the *Journal* was usually published. The newspaper was issued a day earlier, on the Sabbath, because Zenger's sons had been asked to appear in court as witnesses against him. The early publication of the paper also alerted Cosby's enemies that Zenger's trial was starting. Alexander knew that a sympathetic audience in the courtroom might help the case.

Justices DeLancey and Philipse filed into the courtroom in their robes and powdered wigs. Then came the twelve jurors.

Freedom of the Press:
Crown v. John Peter Zenger

Zenger's new lawyer, Andrew Hamilton, disregarded court protocol and addressed the jury himself.

The room was soon filled to capacity with spectators. Attorney General Bradley read the charges and then recited the passages from the *Journal* that were considered seditious libel.

Chambers entered another not-guilty plea for Zenger, and then he started his opening remarks. When he finished, a man in the courtroom stood. The assembly reacted as he identified himself as Andrew Hamilton. Hamilton was a star Philadelphia attorney, known as one of the best lawyers in the colonies. At Alexander's request, Hamilton had come to take over the case from Chambers, who gave him the floor.

The Arguments

Alexander kept the hiring of Hamilton a secret so that Hamilton's appearance would shock the prosecution. Attorney General Bradley had no time to craft an argument questioning Hamilton's ability to serve as Zenger's attorney.

Spectators packed the courtroom during Hamilton's defense of Zenger.

After Hamilton's arrival in New York, Alexander and Smith had worked behind the scenes to prepare him for the trial. They shared all their research and strategies. They believed

Andrew Hamilton

Andrew Hamilton, not to be confused with (nor was he related to) Founding Father Alexander Hamilton, was born in Scotland. He earned his college degree in three years and began studying law at the University of Edinburgh. Hamilton immigrated to America as an indentured servant, an unpaid servant contracted to work for someone for a specific period of time, and worked as a tutor in Virginia. He later moved to Maryland, married, and joined a law firm in England. After returning to America, he became a well-known attorney in Philadelphia. He served in the Pennsylvania General Assembly and was eventually elected speaker, or the person who runs the assembly.

Hamilton was not known for defending freedom of the press. In fact, he had once helped prosecute printer Andrew Bradford, William Bradford's son, for seditious libel. However, he was a friend of James Alexander's. He also liked the challenge of being able to defend any side of an argument. By 1735, he was fifty-nine years old and suffered from gout, a type of painful joint swelling, which made it difficult to travel. Nonetheless, he agreed to come to New York and defend Zenger. Hamilton did not even charge a fee. Today, he is remembered most for his role in Zenger's trial.

Hamilton's status as an outsider could be an advantage in Zenger's trial. He appeared more neutral than the disbarred defense team. Hamilton also was not an ally of either Cosby or Morris.

Hamilton kept to Alexander's plan. He started by making a confession on Zenger's behalf. Hamilton admitted that Zenger was guilty of publishing the papers accused of being seditious libel.

This confession interfered with Bradley's strategy. The attorney general's entire plan had been to prove that Zenger printed the materials in

Hamilton is best remembered for his role in the Zenger trial.

question. After Hamilton admitted it, there was nothing left for Bradley to prove, so he dismissed his witnesses. Bradley addressed the jury. "As Mr. Hamilton has confessed the printing and publishing of these libels," he said, "I think the Jury must find a verdict for the king."

FOUR

Set Free by the Truth

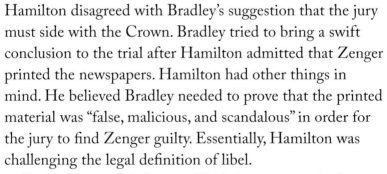

Hamilton disagreed with Bradley's suggestion that the jury must side with the Crown. Bradley tried to bring a swift conclusion to the trial after Hamilton admitted that Zenger printed the newspapers. Hamilton had other things in mind. He believed Bradley needed to prove that the printed material was "false, malicious, and scandalous" in order for the jury to find Zenger guilty. Essentially, Hamilton was challenging the legal definition of libel.

Bradley was startled again. He did not argue whether or not what was printed was true or false. Instead, he restated that it was "a very great offense to speak evil or to revile those in authority over us." He went on to ignore Hamilton's argument and lecture the jury on the reason the government considered seditious libel so dangerous.

The History of Libel Laws

In the trial, Bradley discussed British common law precedents, or legal standards based on previous cases, and reviewed previous libel trials that had ended in guilty verdicts.

He even quoted the Bible to support his point that it was of "great offense" to speak negatively about an authority figure: "For it is written, thou shalt not speak evil of the ruler of thy people." He ended his argument by reading some of the passages Zenger had admittedly printed about Cosby. "If these assertions are not libels, then I don't know what is," Bradley stated.

Hamilton invoked legal precedents like those found in *Opinions on the Crown*, pictured here.

In his response, Hamilton adopted a different tone. "I agree with Mr. Attorney [General] that government is a sacred thing," he said. However, he quickly turned back to his original point. Hamilton argued that men should not have to suffer injustice silently. He believed that speaking out against a bad government should not be a crime. He understood it to be a duty.

Hamilton went on to give a historical review that contrasted Bradley's. He described the Star Chamber as "the most dangerous court to the liberties of the people of England." He reminded jurors that the Star Chamber had long since been abolished. He argued that people in the colonies should not be forced to live by its outdated, overreaching laws. Further, he noted that the governor was neither a monarch nor an elected official of the colony. The colonists did not owe him blind loyalty as they might to the king.

After this, Bradley took the opportunity to repeat his simple argument. The libel laws of the Star Chamber were still the laws of both Britain and the colonies. Hamilton could not dispute that fact. Since the *Journal* had criticized the governor, its articles met the definition of libel. Zenger had acknowledged printing the libelous papers. Therefore, he was guilty of libel. The logic was airtight in Bradley's mind. Whether or not the articles were true was irrelevant.

The official charge against Zenger, however, had referred to the pieces printed in the *Journal* as "false, malicious, seditious and scandalous libel." Hamilton asked the court, "This word 'false' must have some meaning, or else how came it there?" Hamilton urged the jury to consider a definition of libel that reflected the intent of the original slander laws from 1275. "The falsehood makes the scandal, and both make the libel," he argued. In other words, the articles could only be considered libelous if the claims in them were false. Hamilton went on to say that if Bradley could prove that the claims in the paper were false, then Zenger was indeed guilty of libel.

Jury Nullification

Hamilton stubbornly stuck with his line of reasoning. He offered to call new witnesses "to prove those very papers that are called libelous to be true." DeLancey immediately objected, echoing Bradley's legal argument. He believed that "a libel is not to be justified, for it is nevertheless a libel even if it is true." In fact, he reminded Hamilton that true libel was the worst kind under the law because of its increased potential to create public unrest.

DeLancey faced a courtroom packed with angry New Yorkers. The other justice, Philipse, sat quietly and gave

Colonists often rioted to demonstrate their frustrations with the British government. In this image, they are rioting against the British Stamp Act.

authority to his superior. DeLancey knew he would lose control of the crowd if he did not at least make it appear that he was giving Zenger a fair trial. He took time to study the texts that Hamilton, nearly twice his age, suggested that he look at. However, he drew the line at allowing Hamilton to call new witnesses. When Hamilton tried to argue for witnesses again, DeLancey's patience grew thin. He scolded Hamilton, stating that "it is not good manners to insist upon a point in which you are overruled."

Hamilton eventually gave up his plan to call further witnesses. However, he addressed the jury, asking *them* to serve as witnesses to prove the validity of what Zenger had written. The jurors were New Yorkers. They had lived under Cosby's rule. They were qualified, in Hamilton's opinion, to judge whether or not the *Journal*'s articles were true. "In your justice lies our safety," he told them.

37

Hamilton's argument was the same argument Alexander had planned all along. It was a bold one. It was not about what the libel law said. It was about what he believed it should say. Hamilton asked the jury, in essence, to overrule the law of the land. This rare and controversial practice, called jury nullification, meant jurors might return a verdict of "not guilty" when they believed a law was unfair, immoral, or wrong. The effect of the jury's action would be to make the law null and void, or invalid, in that case.

Bushell's Case

The evidence portion of the hearing was over. No witnesses had been called. Hamilton knew his final summary to the jury would likely decide the case. He began this summary by discussing "Bushell's Case." In 1670, Pennsylvania founder William Penn had been tried in England for holding a Quaker prayer meeting in London. At the time, it was illegal to hold a religious meeting that was not associated with the Church of England. Government officials claimed Penn's Quaker meeting disturbed the peace. The judge told the jurors that they had to convict Penn for his crimes. The jurors ignored the judge's instruction and found Penn not guilty. The judge then fined the jurors for disobeying his directions.

One of the jurors, a man named Edward Bushell, refused to pay. He was sent to jail and appealed his conviction. The chief justice ruled in his favor. He wrote that the jury, not the judge, should determine how the law applied to the facts. If jurors could be punished for acting in good faith, he asked, why have them at all?

Zenger's jurors understood that Hamilton was telling this story in order to urge them to act as boldly as Bushell had.

Chief Justice James DeLancey

J ames DeLancey was born in New York City in 1703 into a wealthy and influential colonial family. He attended university in England and was licensed to practice law in 1725 before returning to New York.

Chief Justice James DeLancey later became acting governor of New York.

In 1729, DeLancey became a member of the New York General Assembly. Two years later, he was appointed to the Supreme Court of Judicature. Governor Cosby elevated DeLancey to chief justice in 1733 after he dismissed Lewis Morris. DeLancey was an able and intelligent lawyer, but his loyalty to the governor influenced many of his decisions.

DeLancey later became acting governor of New York. In June 1754, he presided over the Albany Congress, one of the first meetings discussing a union of the American colonies. He died in 1760.

Hamilton asked them to ignore the letter of the law with the hope that justice would ultimately be on their side. Hamilton failed, however, to mention other cases that had not turned out so well for jurors that disobeyed a judge's orders.

Hamilton acknowledged that the jury had the right to do what the judge asked of them. They also had the right not to. They should be free to "determine both the law and the fact," Hamilton argued. If the judge had all the power, the right to have a trial by jury was meaningless.

The Jury's Role

Hamilton then moved on to undercutting the defense of the libel laws. He talked about the Star Chamber again. He spoke of the men who paid dearly for speaking the truth under its rule. He agreed that it was wrong to "scandalize any man." He also stated, however, that those in positions of power had a duty to observe the law. If they did not, then the people must hold them accountable. In other words, he was suggesting that Zenger was holding the governor accountable for his bad behavior.

Hamilton noted how times were different than the times in which the Star Chamber created the libel laws. He said that people in the colonies knew a freedom that was "unheard of in the era of the Star Chamber." For instance, people could exercise religious freedom without fear of being burned at the stake.

To continue this conversation about religion, Hamilton referenced a passage from the Bible that seemed to contradict the one Bradley had shared earlier. From the Book of Isaiah, he read that "the leaders of the people cause them to err, and they that are led by them are destroyed." In other words, people who follow a corrupt government were going to be led

Zenger's case challenged the role of jurors in the court system.

astray. Hamilton was implying that the jurors did not owe the governor their respect if he was guilty of wrongdoings.

The people in the courtroom applauded Hamilton's argument. The colonists knew the dangers of a oppressive ruler. Many of them had come to America in order to flee that type of ruler.

Hamilton concluded by making sure the jurors understood the significance of the decision they were about to make. Hamilton stated:

> The question before the court is not a small or private
> concern. It is not the cause of a poor printer nor of
> New York alone, which you are now trying. No! It may
> in its consequence affect every freeman that lives

Freedom of the Press:
Crown v. John Peter Zenger

Many settlers of the original thirteen colonies were fleeing oppression in their homelands.

under a British government on the main of America. It
is the best cause. It is the cause of liberty.

In other words, Hamilton told the jury that the decision they were making did not just affect Zenger. The decision would affect all of those who lived in the colonies.

After Hamilton's summary, it was Bradley's turn to address the jury. He acknowledged the power of Hamilton's speech. He argued, however, that the cases Hamilton had cited were unrelated to Zenger's case. Therefore, he would not even take the time to disprove Hamilton's arguments. To Bradley, only one fact mattered. Zenger confessed to printing the articles,

42

which clearly criticized the governor. Bradley had "no doubt," he said, that the jury would find the defendant guilty.

A Special Verdict

Finally, it was DeLancey's turn to address the jury. He started by acknowledging that Hamilton's argument might influence the jury to disregard what he was about to say. Even so, he continued.

As Alexander had feared all along, DeLancey instructed the jury to issue a special verdict. He told them to consider only a small set of facts. DeLancey stated that the jury's job was not to determine whether printed material was libelous. He and Philipse had already ruled that it was. If Zenger had indeed printed the materials that he confessed to printing, DeLancey stated, then he must be found guilty.

The jurors left the courtroom to deliberate. Some accounts say they took only ten minutes to reach their verdict. Foreman Thomas Hunt informed the court clerk that they had found the defendant not guilty. The crowd cheered.

Zenger was carried out of the courtroom in celebration of his victory.

FIVE

Freedom of the Press

Chief Justice DeLancey was enraged by the jurors' disregard for his instructions. He had all but ordered the jury to find Zenger guilty. He scolded the crowd for applauding in court and threatened to arrest them.

Over forty supporters threw Hamilton a celebratory dinner that evening at the Black Horse Tavern, across from Zenger's print shop. Zenger was not there. After nine months in jail, he remained behind bars one more night. His supporters raised money so that he could reimburse the city for the cost of his room and board in prison. He was finally freed the next morning.

Not surprisingly, the Cosby-backed *Gazette* printed nothing about the not-guilty verdict in Zenger's trial. Zenger himself published only a short note in the *Journal*: "The printer, having got his liberty again, designs God willing to finish and publish the charter of the City of New York next week." Zenger was back to business as usual.

The ships in the harbor fired their cannons in a congratulatory gun salute as Hamilton set sail to return

> CONGRESS SHALL MAKE NO LAW *respecting an establishment of religion, or prohibiting the free exercise thereof; or abridging the freedom of speech, or of the press; or the right of the people peaceably to assemble, and to petition the Government for a redress of grievances.*
>
> 🍎 **THE FIRST AMENDMENT TO THE U.S. CONSTITUTION**
> 15 DECEMBER 1791

The First Amendment to the US Constitution established freedom of the press.

to Philadelphia. Out of gratitude, New York's mayor and aldermen presented Hamilton with an engraved gold box. It read: "Gained not by money but by virtue." The city also issued a decree praising Hamilton's "learned and generous defense of the rights of mankind, and the liberty of the press."

Aftermath

Fearful of revenge by Governor Cosby, the people of New York downplayed their excitement over the Zenger verdict. In the weeks that followed, Cosby's hold on power seemed as strong as ever. However, his fortunes soon turned.

In November, Morris successfully persuaded the London Privy Council that Cosby had unfairly removed him from his judgeship. Cosby defended his actions. While Morris was not reinstated as chief justice, the king apologized for Cosby's unjust behavior.

Soon after, Cosby fell ill with tuberculosis. He was bedridden for four months. As he attempted to maintain his power, the people of New York rebelled. Alexander resumed publishing anti-Cosby articles in the *Journal*. He knew how truly powerful the press could be. He had an idea to make it even more influential.

The Zenger verdict had inspired New Yorkers to challenge Cosby's authority. If Alexander published an account of the trial, then he could draw more attention to that moment in history. Perhaps those who opposed Cosby could regain political momentum against him. Maybe they could even have him removed as governor.

It turned out that step was unnecessary. Cosby died in March 1736. The same day Cosby died, Alexander received Hamilton's notes on the Zenger trial for inclusion in a book Alexander was writing. In June, under Zenger's byline, or name, Alexander published *A Brief Narrative of the Case and Trial of John Peter Zenger, Printer of the New-York Weekly Journal*. The forty-page pamphlet detailed the Zenger case. It was widely read in New York. It was also reprinted in Boston and circulated throughout the colonies. Five editions were printed in London. Thanks to Alexander's account, Zenger's case earned its place in history as one of the most famous trials of the colonial era.

In 1738, Benjamin Franklin's *Pennsylvania Gazette* reported that the Zenger trial was being discussed in every coffee house in London. "Our political writers of different factions, who never agreed in anything else, have mentioned the trial in their public writings with an air of rapture and triumph," the reporter wrote. "We look upon Zenger's advocate as a glorious asserter of public liberty." In other

In the early 1900s, New Yorkers celebrated Zenger's courtroom victory with a parade float depicting the trial.

words, writers who were often divided on certain issues were all celebrating the Zenger victory. They also agreed that Hamilton was a great defender of liberty.

Meanwhile, the British had appointed a new royal governor of New York: George Clarke. He was a Cosby supporter. Cosby's enemies were sure he would make their lives miserable. However, Clarke sensed the public's dislike of Cosby. He made the wise political choice to call for new and fair elections. Lewis Morris and his son were returned to the legislature. Alexander was readmitted to the bar and reappointed to the New York Governor's Council. John Peter Zenger also replaced William Bradford as New York's royal printer.

Zenger continued publishing the *Journal* until he died at age forty-nine in 1746. His wife, Anna, continued producing the

paper for two years after his death. She then turned it over to Zenger's eldest son. The last issue of the *Journal* was published in 1751, nearly twenty years after the paper's first issue.

Legal Implications

The jury in Zenger's case had ignored existing libel laws to find Zenger not guilty. In the aftermath of the trial, however, the libel law remained in effect. Nonetheless, Zenger's case had important long-term effects. It highlighted the importance of freedom of the press. It also showed the power of a jury in the justice system.

While written criticism of the government remained illegal, Zenger's trial brought new respect to journalism and helped elevate its importance in society. Political writing was now considered a valid form of political expression. Writers grew more comfortable writing critically over time. By the time the British Stamp Act was introduced in 1765, many newspapers were openly critical of the British government. The act itself, which taxed printed material in the colonies, was a major factor in pushing America to declare its independence from England.

The Bill of Rights

At the conclusion of the Revolutionary War in 1783, the American colonies were freed from British rule. While the new American legal system was based on British law, it differed in several important ways.

Initially, the US Constitution provided no guaranteed freedom of the press. At the Constitutional Convention in 1787, Pennsylvania statesman Gouverneur Morris brought up the Zenger trial. He called the trial "the germ of American

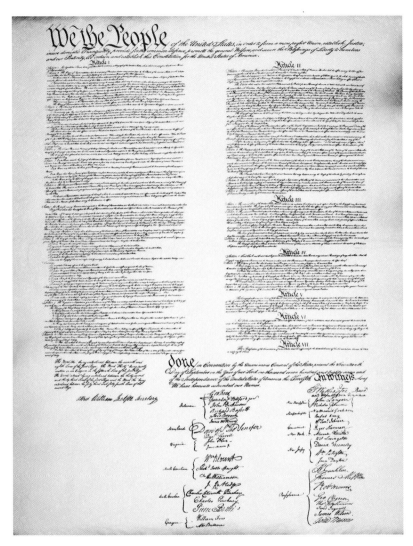

The original US Constitution did not guarantee freedom of the press.

freedom, the morning star of that liberty which subsequently revolutionized America." In other words, he thought that the liberty demonstrated through the Zenger trial was one of the founding principles of America.

49

The Bill of Rights was written in 1789. It contains the first ten amendments, or additions, to the Constitution. Within the Bill of Rights, the First Amendment guarantees basic freedoms to the American people. Freedom of speech and freedom of the press are among those basic freedoms, as is the right to peacefully assemble.

The Sedition Act

The United States became the first country to guarantee free speech. However, this freedom had limits. In 1798, President John Adams and the Federalist Party, his political party, passed the Alien and Sedition Acts. Like the Star Chamber laws, these laws made it a crime to publish "false, scandalous, and malicious writing" against the government. Adams claimed these laws were necessary while the United States was at odds with France. He thought any negativity about the government would weaken national security. However, he and his allies primarily used the Sedition Act to silence his critics, who supported Vice President Thomas Jefferson and the Democratic-Republican Party.

Jefferson's friend James Madison, who would go on to become president, criticized the Sedition Act as an American version of the British libel laws. He argued that they violated the intent of the First Amendment. Adams's attempt to silence opposing viewpoints was unpopular. Americans voted him out of office and elected Jefferson as their next president. Before the Sedition Act could be challenged before the Supreme Court, Jefferson allowed it to expire in 1801.

Ironically, Jefferson grew frustrated when the press began attacking him. A Virginia journalist and Jefferson supporter named James Callender made his career printing

mean-spirited stories about many of Jefferson's enemies. For instance, he wrote negative articles about John Adams and Alexander Hamilton.

Thomas Jefferson supported journalists' attacks on his enemies, including Alexander Hamilton, pictured here.

Jefferson secretly supported Callender's attacks on his political enemies. Eventually, Callender was arrested and prosecuted under the Sedition Act. He went to jail for nine months. When he was released, he expected that Jefferson would repay him by giving him a job. When Jefferson failed to do so, Callender was angry. In Callender's frustration, he wrote a series of negative articles about Jefferson and his relationship with an enslaved woman named Sally Hemings.

The Future of the First Amendment and Freedom of the Press

Although Jefferson let the Sedition Act expire, there have been other cases in American history that have threatened people's First Amendment rights. In 1927, Minnesota officials used a public nuisance law to stop a newspaper published by Jay Near from publishing future articles that were critical of the state government. The law allowed state officials to put an end to the publication of a "malicious, scandalous and defamatory newspaper, magazine or other

periodical" if it was found to be "guilty of a nuisance," or annoyance. Near challenged this law. When the case made it to the US Supreme Court in 1931 (*Near v. Minnesota ex rel. Olson*), the justices ruled that it was unconstitutional to censor or prohibit the publication of the newspaper before

The Future of Libel Laws in New York

O ne young writer named Harry Croswell published a Federalist paper called the *Wasp* in New York. Croswell published articles that stated that Thomas Jefferson paid editor James Callendar to publish attacks against his political rivals, including George Washington and John Adams. Jefferson denied these claims. He encouraged the state to prosecute Croswell for libel. Croswell was convicted. When he appealed the verdict, Jefferson's nemesis, Alexander Hamilton, stepped in to represent him.

As Andrew Hamilton did in the Zenger trial, Alexander Hamilton used truth as a defense against the libel claims. While Hamilton did not win the case, Croswell was granted a new trial. The new trial was never rescheduled.

In the aftermath, however, New York incorporated Hamilton's argument into a new law. In 1805, New York made it a law that factual written statements could no longer be considered libel in the state.

The New York Times

LATE CITY EDITION

VOL. CXXIII—No. 42,508

NEW YORK, FRIDAY, AUGUST 9, 1974

15 CENTS

NIXON RESIGNS

HE URGES A TIME OF 'HEALING'; FORD WILL TAKE OFFICE TODAY

'Sacrifice' Is Praised; Kissinger to Remain

The 37th President Is First to Quit Post

SPECULATION RIFE ON VICE PRESIDENT

POLITICAL SCENE — *Rise and Fall*

JAWORSKI ASSERTS NO DEAL WAS MADE

Appraisal of Nixon Career

President Nixon resigned after newspaper reporters exposed information that portrayed him in a bad light.

it was actually published. This decision established that prior restraint, or prepublication censorship, was illegal.

The US Supreme Court upheld this decision in 1971 after President Richard Nixon tried to force the *New York Times* and the *Washington Post* to stop publishing classified material about the Vietnam War. Nixon claimed that national security was threatened by the publication of information about the United States' involvement in the war. Yet again, the Supreme Court determined that this type of censorship was unconstitutional.

Despite the fact that there have been challenges of the First Amendment, freedom of the press still remains one of this country's long-standing principles. The *Crown v. John Peter Zenger* case was a crucial first step to securing freedom of speech and freedom of the press in this country.

Chronology

1735 A jury in the colony of New York rules that John Peter Zenger is not guilty of seditious libel. Although this does not set a legal precedent concerning seditious libel or establish freedom of the press, it sets a foundation for these concepts (*Crown v. John Peter Zenger*).

1791 The First Amendment to the US Constitution, which protects freedom of speech and freedom of the press, is ratified, or made official.

1805 New York State writes into law that truth is a defense against libel. This law is a result of *People v. Croswell* (1804).

1931 The Supreme Court rules that prior restraint of publication is unconstitutional (*Near v. Minnesota ex rel. Olson*).

1964 The Supreme Court rules that a libel conviction requires "actual malice" on the part of the defendant. In other words, the defendant had to publish the material in question without regard to whether it was true or with knowledge that it was false (*New York Times Company v. Sullivan*).

1971 The Supreme Court upholds its previous ruling that prior restraint is unconstitutional (*New York Times Company v. United States*).

1972 The Supreme Court rules that reporters cannot use the First Amendment to avoid testifying before a grand jury (*Branzburg v. Hayes*).

1988 The Supreme Court rules that public school administrators can censor student-run newspapers because they are part of the school curriculum (*Hazelwood School District v. Kuhlmeier*).

Glossary

amendment An addition to a legal document.

attorney general The chief lawyer for a government.

censorship The prohibition of certain material.

co-counsel A lawyer who helps another attorney represent a client.

defamation An act that damages someone else's reputation.

disbar To take away someone's right to practice law.

First Amendment The first addition to the US Constitution. It ensures every citizen's right to freedom of speech, freedom of the press, freedom of religion, and the freedom to peacefully assemble.

grand jury A group of jurors selected to decide whether or not a case should be taken to trial.

habeas corpus A law that lets defendants object to being held in prison illegally.

indict To make formal charges against someone.

jury nullification A jury delivering a not-guilty verdict because they disagree with the law or the punishment of the law in question.

libel A written defamation.

malicious Intending to cause harm.

plea A formal statement of guilt or innocence before a court.

precedent Earlier legal cases that influence the application of a particular law.

prior restraint Government censorship of material before publication.

recuse To excuse oneself from making a decision because of a conflict of interest.

seditious Inciting rebellion against a state or monarch.

slander A verbal defamation.

sue To file a lawsuit against someone because of unfair treatment.

Further Information

Books

Edelman, Rob. *Freedom of the Press.* Issues on Trial. San Diego: Greenhaven Press, 2007.

Gibson, Karen Bush. *The Life and Times of John Peter Zenger.* Profiles in American History. Hockessin, DE: Mitchell Lane Publishers, Inc., 2007.

Harris, Duchess, and Kari A. Cornell. *Freedom of the Press.* American Values and Freedoms. Minneapolis: ABDO Group, 2017.

Jarrow, Gail. *The Printer's Trial: The Case of John Peter Zenger and the Fight for a Free Press.* Honesdale, PA.: Calkins Creek, 2006.

Websites

The Constitutional Rights Foundation: The Trial of John Peter Zenger
http://www.crf-usa.org/images/pdf/znger_ms.pdf

This website gives information about the history of libel law and includes discussion questions and activities.

Newseum: The Birth of Press Freedom

http://www.newseum.org/2014/11/18/the-birth-of-press-freedom

This web page describes an exhibit about John Peter Zenger at the Newseum in Washington, DC.

The Trial of John Peter Zenger: A Play in Five Scenes by Michael E. Tigar

https://scholarship.law.duke.edu/cgi/viewcontent.cgi?referer=https://www.google.com/&httpsredir=1&article=6394&context=faculty_scholarship

This play, written for the American Bar Association, gives a dramatic account of the Zenger trial.

Videos

Freedom of the Press: Crash Course Government and Politics

https://www.youtube.com/watch?v=Vtpd0EbaFoQ

This educational video is an introduction to freedom of the press.

Studio One: The Trial of John Peter Zenger

https://www.youtube.com/watch?v=uDGIgF3VAto

This classic teleplay from 1953 depicts Zenger's trial.

Unexpected Verdict: The Trial of John Paul Zenger

https://www.youtube.com/watch?v=Ab8lPjHIkoI

This is an award-winning student video made for National History Day.

Selected Bibliography

Amponsah, Peter Nkrumah. *Libel Law, Political Criticism, and Defamation of Public Figures: The United States, Europe and Australia*. New York: LFB Scholarly Publishing LLC, 2010.

Barnett, Lincoln. "The Case of John Peter Zenger." *American Heritage* 23, no. 1 (December 1971). http://www.americanheritage.com/content/case-john-peter-zenger.

Burns, Eric. *Infamous Scribblers: The Founding Fathers and the Rowdy Beginnings of American Journalism*. New York: PublicAffairs, 2007.

Copeland, David A. *Debating the Issues in Colonial Newspapers: Primary Documents on Events of the Period*. Westport, CT: Greenwood Publishing Group, 2000.

Costly, Andrew. "The Rule of Law in Dangerous Times: John Peter Zenger and Freedom of the Press." Constitutional Rights Foundation, Fall 2006. http://www.crf-usa.org/bill-of-rights-in-action/bria-22-3-b-john-peter-zenger-and-freedom-of-the-press.

"Crown v. John Peter Zenger." Historical Society of the New York Courts. Accessed December 7, 2017. http://www.nycourts.gov/history/legal-history-new-york/legal-history-eras-01/history-new-york-legal-eras-crown-zenger.html.

Fleming, Thomas. "Verdicts of History IV: 'A Scandalous, Malicious, and Seditious Libel.'" *American Heritage* 19, no. 1 (December 1967). http://www.americanheritage.com/content/verdicts-history-iv"-scandalous-malicious-and-seditious-libel".

Kluger, Richard. *Indelible Ink: The Trials of John Peter Zenger and the Birth of America's Free Press.* New York: W. W. Norton & Company, 2017.

Magnet, Myron. "How American Press Freedom Began on Wall Street." *City Journal*, Autumn 2010. http://www.city-journal.org/html/how-american-press-freedom-began-wall-street-13336.html.

McGratch, Paul. "People v. Croswell: Alexander Hamilton and the Transformation of the Common Law of Libel." *Judicial Notice* 7 (Summer 2011). http://www.nycourts.gov/history/programs-events/images/Judicial-Notice-07.pdf#page=6.

Rutherford, Livingston. *John Peter Zenger: His Press, His Trial, and a Bibliography of Zenger Imprints.* Classic Reprint Series. London: Forgotten Books, 2015.

Volokh, Eugene. "Alexander Hamilton, the Truth, and Freedom of the Press." *Washington Post*, June 28, 2016. http://www.washingtonpost.com/news/volokh-conspiracy/wp/2016/06/28/alexander-hamilton-the-truth-and-freedom-of-the-press/?utm_term=.27e44a97539a.

Index

About the Author

Jeanne Marie Ford is an Emmy Award–winning television scriptwriter. She holds an MFA in writing for children from Vermont College. She has written numerous books and articles on a variety of subjects. She also teaches college English. She lives in Maryland with her husband and two children.